Quilless

an Astrological Journey
of Poetry & Wordcraft

Quilless

An Astrological Journey
of Poetry & Wordcraft

Cheryl Anne Ruebner

Mending Moon/Wicked Owl Press

Thank you to...

My Mother Carole Rosa, for giving me birth, and a case of freshly sharpened pencils on my first day of school. I was thrilled to learn to write.

My Stepfather Peter Rosa, for enthusiastically attending my first Poetry Feature, and for uncountable "sunk costs."

James Cassidy, for always being there as a well of support, and very literally funding my groceries and keeping me alive so this book could be published.

Walker East-West, for tremendous support and encouragement for me to follow my Soul Child and focus on my writing.

Johanna O'Tigham, for literal, relational, clerical, and magical support during some of my toughest times

Furesø Libraries of Copenhagen, Denmark. You issued me, a foreigner on a travel visa, a library card and made it possible for me to complete this work. I'll be forever grateful for your unknowing contribution.

rm, for the use of your hammock that sheltered me while I completed and published this project

and for tech support, in alphabetical order:

AdmFubar, ajlittoz, a.l.e, Mimi Alonso, Rhonda Buttery, EarnestAI, Filip Arsić, Tom Callanan, Upasika Deva, Martina Eskirne, Mary Hart, Madeline Hillis-Dineen, Miguel Etchepare, Julia JS, PatJr, Pixlab, Polygon, rich2005, Laurien Rueger, sallyanne, sersha, Paul Scaturro, Nancy Schorr, William Thompson, utnik, Dougie van der Beak, Milja Wi

Table of Contents

Foreword

Concept in Context: Autobiographical Background

The concept of this book came to me after the few years it covers had passed. I had not known that I'd become so serious about Astrology; I had only been saving the timestamps of the poems because I'd been posting them immediately after completion on my Wordpress blog, which was named Quilless/quilless (though was also pretty particular about it, as though I knew they would be important). I don't remember when the idea first came, but it was likely after I'd spent a few years hardcore on the Rainbow Trail and put myself through the International Academy of Astrology's Natal Astrology Certificate program. At the time, I was more interested in Living My Life to the (sometimes totally over the top) fullest than I was in publishing. Eventually, though, the inspiration came to put the two together. It would be a few years, and another few after that, including multiple stalled starts and re-dos, before the project could root and stand.

The years covered by this collection begin right before I dropped out of Graduate School (in order to "become a poet," of course) and end two seasons after my first Rainbow Gathering. During this span is when I experienced my first Saturn Return; the chronology is very literally, therefore, a poetic and astrological journey through my journey into the first layers of Adulthood. I was 25 at the moment of the first poem in the collection, and 30 at the last. I'd been studying Astrology on my own, but my proper education came later.

This book is at once a Poetry Collection and an exercise in Astrological Practice. Personally, I see it as a delayed self-assigned "final project" for the IAA course. I didn't move forward with the Professional Education program (with the exception of completing Ethics), and so I was let out into the world without a sense of true closure.

I had to go my own way and create my own path, and yet I didn't feel as though my own personal retrospective of that time period was complete without tying it all up and letting it go. I feel as though this project has allowed me to weave an integration of this period between two of pillars of my life, while offering an intriguing twist on both genres. I am happy that I've treated two dogs with one bone by doing so.

Recordkeeping & Timestamp Accuracy

I'd generally timestamped the poems either immediately after they came (if I was at the computer at the moment), or very shortly thereafter (if I wasn't). There is often conjecture in the Astrological community about when a document is "birthed," but the general consensus is that it is when it cannot be undone, when it is "signed." So, even though a blog entry can be edited, and even the timestamp changed, I am noting the moment of its "cementing" in the realm of public access (digital publication) as canonical. A good example of this is "defrosting in the brisk…" which was scribed with pen before dusk, but published online in the middle of the night. It's the only timestamp I have, so it must do. And so it is with the others; I've worked with what I have had.

Integrating the Astrology: Methodology and Limitations

As mentioned before, the poems of this collection came first, and the collection is meant to stand on its own even without the Astrological integration. But, here we are having integrated it. What does this mean, exactly?

A natal (birth) chart can be made for anything: of course: a birth of a physical body (usually one of our own species, but any body, classically one that takes a breath), a birth of a company, a birth of a country, a document, an idea… or a work of art.

However, reading the birth chart of a poem is not like reading the birth chart of a person or of a company, or even of a worldly event. The first type evolves: a person is sentient, grows physically and metaphysically, lives a life; a company goes through changes, ups and downs of finance and market success... but a work of art has none of these qualities. It may be presented (in many different ways), discussed, and shared, but it doesn't have the same concerns as these other forms of entities do, and therefore its birth chart must be interpreted differently. I found myself in the midst of an experiment: how would I read the charts, and what would I find?

Two factors presented as important: methodology, and the natural limitations set in place by the format of the book. The limitations were essentially that the astrology portion would only take up a certain physical area of the book, which worked out to be one page per poem: sometimes this is equal to what the poem itself was given, but never more. It was always important that the book be a Poetry Collection at its core. After the chart itself, the remaining space to delineate (analyze) was very limited, and so I've bent conventions to fit as much information in a small space as possible, without using Astrological Glyphs. However, the glyphs are shown in the Key so that readers who are new to Astrology can glean information from the charts.

Methodology came next. I wanted the astrological writing to support the poems, intrigue folks who already understand Astrologuese, and gently educate those who don't but are open to learning. I also knew that due to the natural limitations, my approach had to be relatively superficial. And, I accepted that there was no way for me to be unbiased: as the author of the poems, I know them very well, and have my own personal and literary perspectives on them, which I then naturally looked for in the charts. In this way, one could say that I have "cherry picked". To that I say that I could not have done anything else! The goal, was, in fact, to look for delicious ripe cherries, to pick out correlations and present them as fascinating "food for thought," to demonstrate how one may read a chart and find how every thing born in this reality is woven into a perfect synchronistic fabric. I am absolutely not claiming any scientific or clinical rigor in this book. Rather, my methodology here is artistic.

On the Constellational Zodiac

Adept chartreaders may notice right away that I have chosen to use a dual zodiac wheel both showing the Tropical signs (what most Westerners learn) and the Constellational signs (the actual constellations in the sky). I also reference some of the Constellational positions in my delineations. Including the Constellational Zodiac may be a point of contention for certain practitioners, and yet, this is how I often cast my charts for my own use. I believe that even if we're speaking in Tropical terms, that keeping in mind what our Eyes see when we observe the sky directly is crucial for remaining grounded in our reality and spiritually connected to the Cosmos.

Biographical Weaving

It was a natural consequence of looking at charts of moments of the "births" of my own artworks for my first book that I would find many correlations with my own natal chart. This is a natural phenomenon: any person's chart will be activated by the charts of important moments in their life. However, I did not expect some of the rare arrangements that ended up being present. At times they were uncanny. For instance, "oroborus" emerged, of all days, on the exact first instance of my Saturn Return, a one-day affair. And then there was "defrosting in the brisk..." which has quite a few remarkable alignments; incidentally, this poem was the only one in this collection to happen in a trance that I had no control over. One can read just as much about the poem as about its significance in the authors' life by looking at these alignments.

To respect the limitations of the book's scope, I have not printed biwheels. Rather, for Chart-Readers who are interested in investigating the correlations, I'm including my own natal chart here. Of course, publishing one's own chart is also sometimes an initiatory ritual for an Astrologer in and of itself. It is an act of transparency and good faith. I can't help but do it anyway, with my Tropical Mercury in Leo.

Cheryl Anne Ruebner's Natal Chart

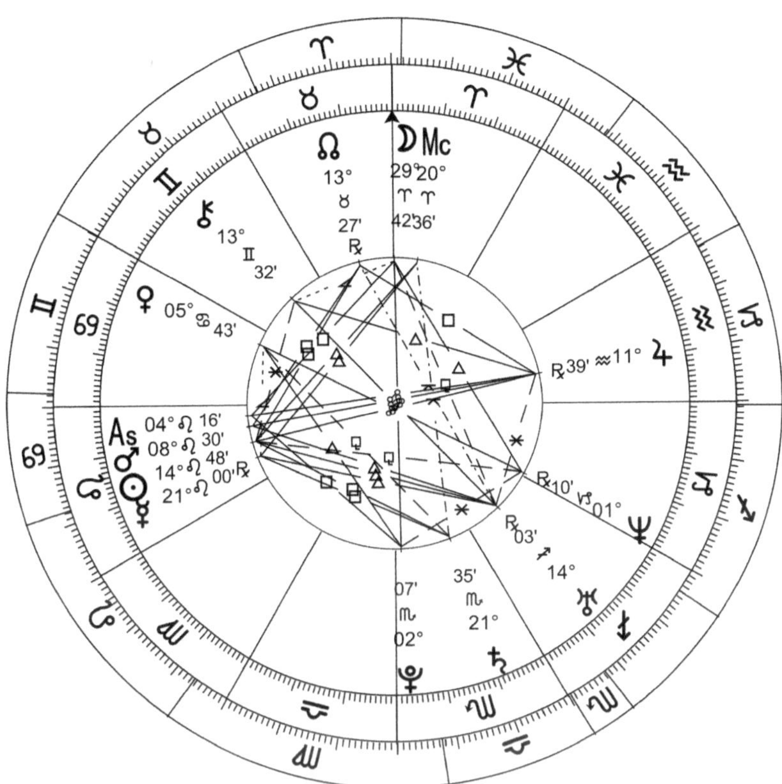

I hope that you enjoy this collection. It's been thirteen years in the making to bring it to your hands.

With love,

Cheryl Anne

Key

Glyphs

♈	Aries	☉	Sun
♉	Taurus	☽	Moon
♊	Gemini	☿	Mercury
♋	Cancer	♀	Venus
♌	Leo	♂	Mars
♍	Virgo	♃	Jupiter
♎	Libra	♄	Saturn
♏	Scorpio	♅	Uranus
♐	Sagittarius	♆	Neptune
♑	Capricorn	♇	Pluto
♒	Aquarius	⚷	Chiron
♓	Pisces		

May 5, 2011 at 09:05 Sound Beach NY

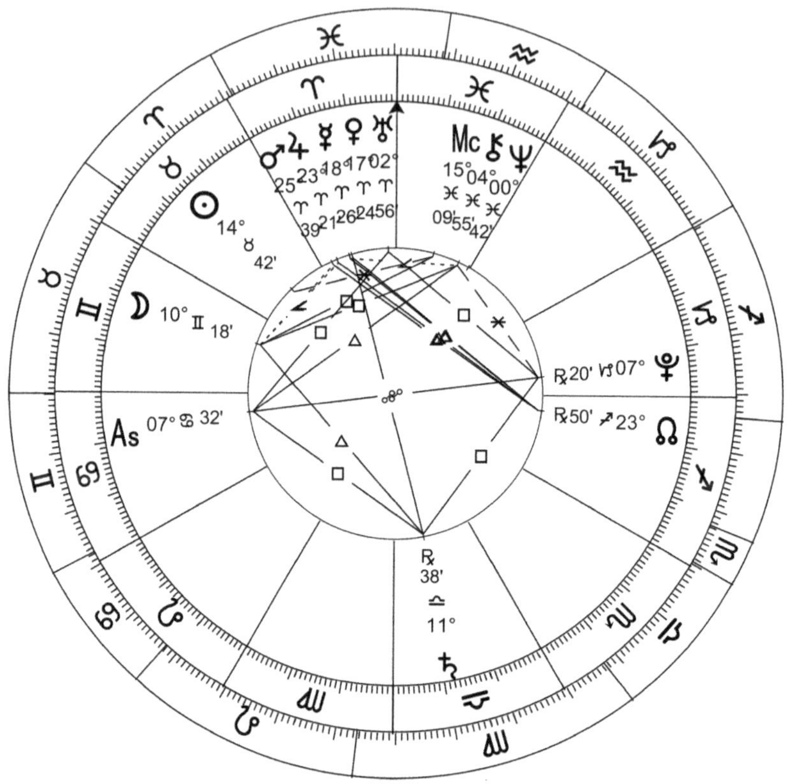

My eyes see first the lone Saturn, then the opposing stellium (group of planets). There's a whopping rare 5 planets together there in Tropical Aries & Constellational Pisces. How interesting that the poem's two major images are fire & water, the elements of those two signs. Air/wind & Earth are also mentioned in the poem, but less often.

The translation of the chart arrangement to the poem continues with more literal imagery: Mercury represents Hands & is in the sign of Tropical Aries (A Fire Started), flanked immediately by two bodies on each side. Saturn opposing it all gives a threat of snuffing, or "death," in the Air sign of Libra. Later, we see the opposite hands holding items, represented by the planets flanking Mercury further away: either a candle (Sun), or Saline (Saltwater, ruled by Neptune). Pluto on the Descendant represents the powerful significance of the partner.

we hold candles in our hands.

but don't let them flicker in the wind

for fear of letting them die.

would you have the courage to lift them up?

would you have the courage to let that flame thrive on its own?

I'll say that your wax has dried here.

and flaking off,

your fingerprints are only imprints in the waves

under my toes

imperceptible to the flames.

the lava I held there on my breast sits separate as a relic.

ancient pools lie right outside.

in one hand our fragile taper.

and out of one saline.

I am standing nude on a primordial beach.

The sandbar alights in an ancient blaze.

the contract

May 10, 2011 at 09:45   Port Jefferson NY

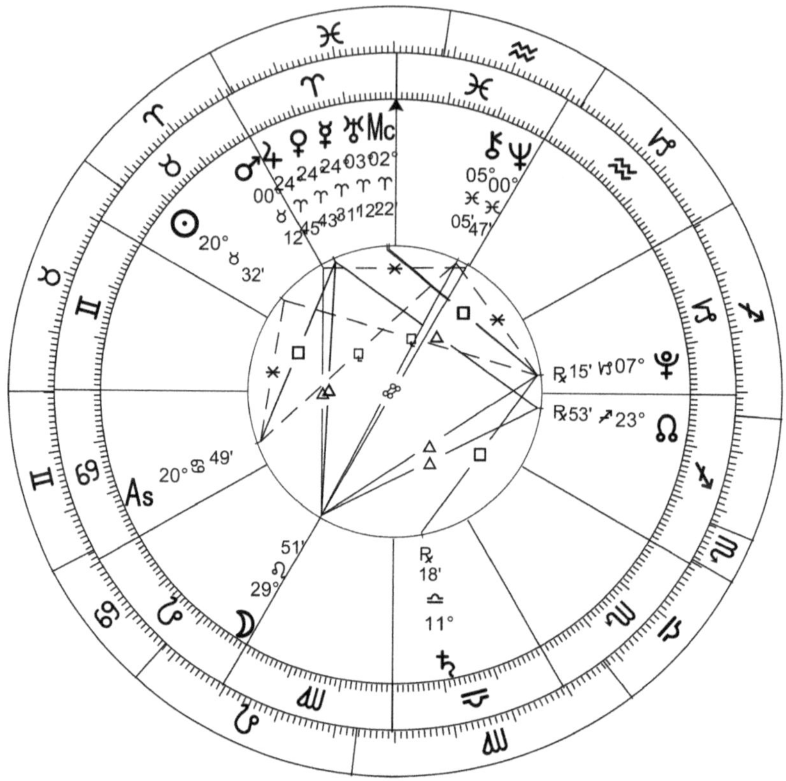

Here Tropical Mars has moved into earthy Taurus, so the blazing fires of Aries are tempered, but the action-oriented masculinity of Mars leading the planet sequence is more pronounced due to the sign change. It comes through strong with the motorcycle image. The Moon is Void of Course (separating from its last possible major aspect), which is classically the best time to conduct any clandestine activity (as the narrator is clearly clearly involved with). Moon is in a Tropical out-of-sign opposition with Neptune (in Leo, symbolizing hair), which well explains the changeability of the narrator, and more notably the heavy nihilistic tone. The extremely tight conjunction between Mercury, Venus, and Jupiter, absolutely the chart's most powerful factor, sets the stage for a successful mission having to do with money. Their trine with the North Node supports the act being somehow fated or ordained. Meanwhile, the Saturn opposition here balances the success of the mission with the nihilism of the finale.

"rent a motorcycle for the inconspicuous license plate.

drive to poughkeepsie and stroll into a dive bar."

I've dyed my hair

and I've bought my jewelry at the gas station.

and then I locate the loner stoner who drinks whiskey

because he knows I know he knows where to find what I need.

the mission isn't complete until I return home

cash deposit returned. five hundred dollars in my pocket,

barely stuffed in next to what I came for.

this assignment is a spiritual contract.

after too many whiskeys and revelations

we must sign our scribbles in the dust.

five hundred dollar bills fall out of my pocket and it doesn't matter.

drafts through the reeds

July 19, 2011 at 05:14   Riverhead NY

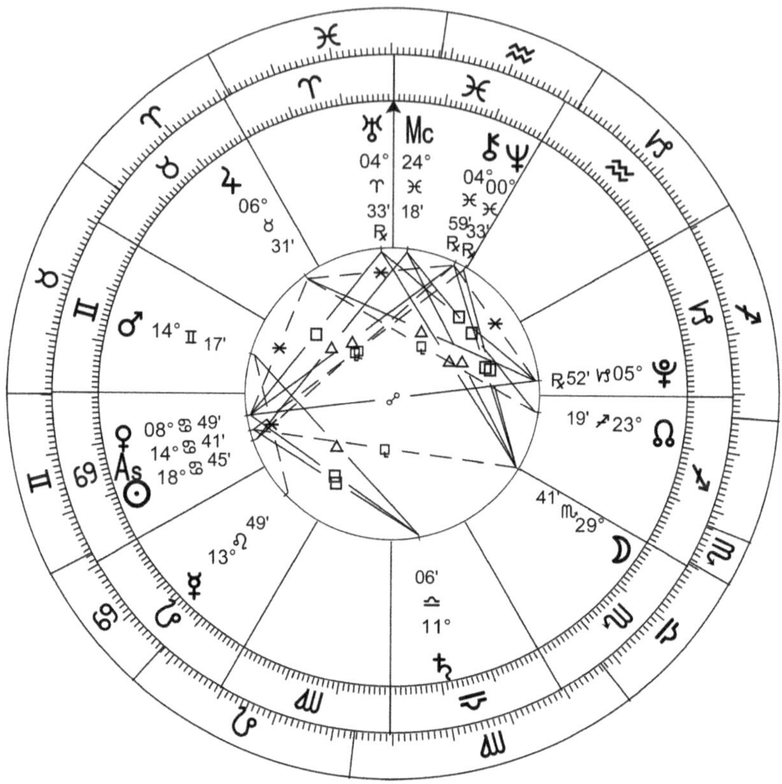

Here we have the Sun rising, marking a sense of newness & promise. Venus as Morning Star has already risen, bringing the themes of relationality and enjoyment to the forefront. She is in Tropical Cancer (being by the water) and Constellational Gemini (two companions, and the themes of language, duality, and communication). The Moon is at the final and most prominent degree of Scorpio, which is "fixed water:" in the poem this is literally "murky water." The Anaretic degree represents a full expansion of the sign into transmutation, which for murky water would be, of course, a lotus flower. In this case, I wrote about fernflowers to the same metaphor: we don't even have to know about what's underneath, as the transmutation into the light has already happened.

Uranus at the Midheaven signifies revelation: it's not enough that the moment is blissful: we also experience a flash of insight from the Soul.

alone with my companion.

with my companion, alone.

I am alone. he is alone, and we are alone together.

the earth whispers to us a song in many languages.

some only one of us hear.

but we hear a lot of them together.

the purple spiral fiddlehead fern flowers blossom,

infused and doused,

out of the murky warmcoolwarm surface of silk water.

within minutes we are native humans.

sitting, thinking, communicating silently.

gathering, assembling, waiting patiently.

discovering, praying, celebrating in unity.

bask in the ocean, for it cleanses you.

let the birds come in, for they sing for you.

swim in the sun, for it feeds you.

dance in the trees, for they tell you the truth.

the gradient

September 12, 2011 at 05:05   Medford NY

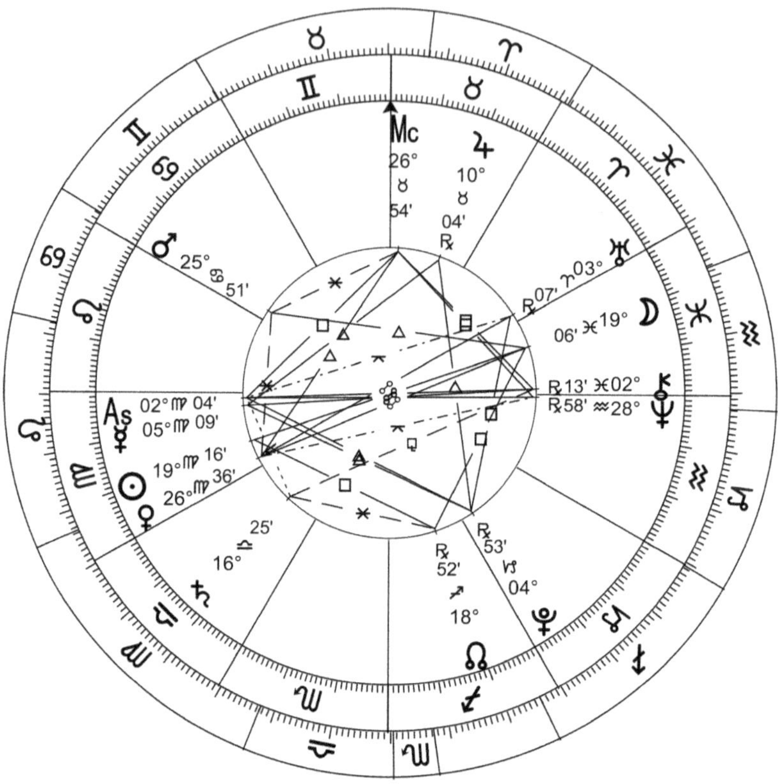

Here we are at the very peak of the full Moon, and moving through imagery on backdrops of three shades of blue sky. The moon is in Tropical Pisces, a Water sign, or Constellational Aquarius, the Water Bearer, and the colors we see are all of water...until they aren't. A Yod between Venus and Mars flanking the Ascendant, with Neptune and Chiron at the point, quite literally brings to mind one female and one male observing a phantasmagoria in the heavens, but in a way that is inherently unfulfilled: "it would be the same there too," no matter how grandiose and wonderful it feels in the meantime.

Breaking down the Yod we have two Quincuni, an aspect that demonstrates "things not matching up or seeing each other." Indeed, both the beauty we see (Venus) and the fire in the sky (Mars) are somehow not fully in alignment with what we must surrender to (Neptune).

the sky bleeds cornflower blue perfectly like that crayola color. we wait in waiting; we sit and fall sleepy in fall-fever season. smoking cigarettes against our better judgment there's a thought of calm anticipation, like one or both of us has a dream or many and it's just a matter of time until the new moon comes up in the right sign or an anonymous benefactor dotes on us or we reach the perfect threshold of substances, laughter, or musing.

the sky is puffing indigo and the question comes up of joint fire or double-helix power and captain planet makes me chuckle. the crickets really begin to speak now at twilight and although their song makes perfect sense, it's not of our language and the tragedy is that like all other beauty in this world the translation is transitory. forgotten as soon as the babel fish bloops it out.

now the sky is seething, floating in royal blue and although the silence and breathing is lapping over and under there's a dis-settlement, as though we aren't meant to be here under the blue but instead under the red, fire sky, scratched up by black obsidian, a different breed of locust calling out not to us at all, laughing and scoffing at that gall of ours to sing back.

it would be the same there too.

affinity

September 14, 2011 at 06:29   Port Jefferson NY

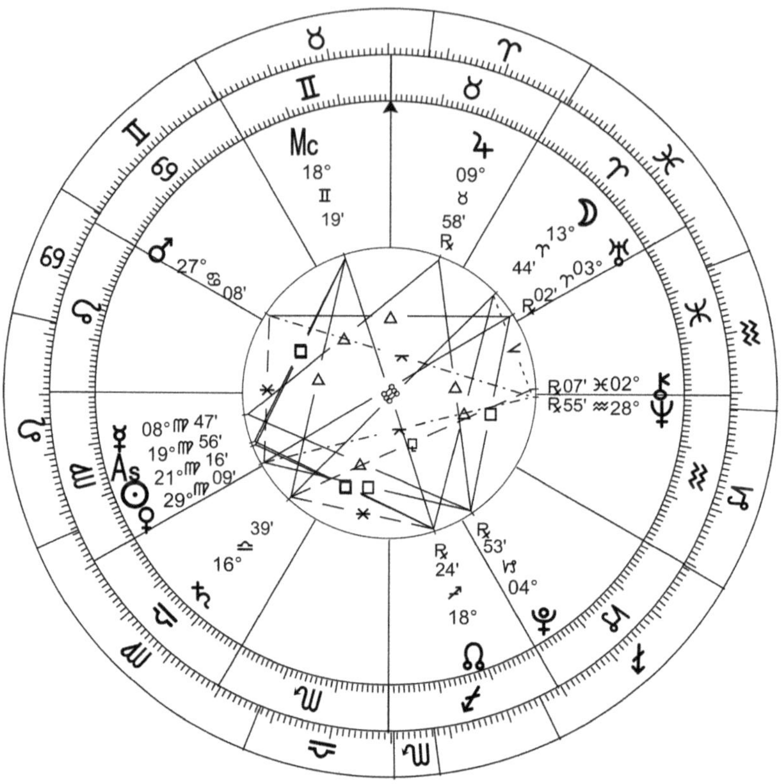

With a title like "affinity," the first thing I did was look for notable conjunctions. Although there is one between Sun and Mercury, it's too wide to consider. And, there are no Antiscias. So, I looked for Mutual Receptions (two planets being in each others' signs), and found Mars and Moon. This creates an "accidental affinity" (a play on the technical term "accidental dignity"). In this case, it represents that the feelings (Moon) and passions (Mars) of the moment support each other. Mars usually would want to separate, but here that energy goes toward unification.

Venus at the anaretic (final) degree of Virgo and just coming out of being combust (burnt) by the Sun shows the precision of the colors being mixed for a painting: the deliberate intention for a beautiful thing is able to be seen. Finally, The Moon is a little less than a day past Full, and could be said to be literally doing what is described in the last line.

there's an acute danger in affinity.

just as with any two things that are the same.

mathematics understands this as exponential growth.

we know it as pouring water into a full tub,

or too much pressure on the one side of a glass,

or a tidal wave responding to a small-scale quake on the coast of a small

town.

we pray for a counter.

opposites aren't much better, though,

an even-steven leaves all factors at zero,

and a balance beam balanced, though beautiful in its lesson of

equilibrium, can impart no progress through its stagnation.

but there's an acute threat of fate in affinity's innate shades and shadows.

we understand as one of our most basic tenets that each set of eyes might

not see the same as the other.

voted for as though in alliance, bakers understand this well.

like sifting fine powders, rising and settling suddenly makes more sense.

a given color is mixed into all points of that palette, said the painter to

me when I asked her the secret of hue over a glass of Montalcino.

the blood red of the sun over the post-apocalyptic village
is in every house,
every window,
even the shades of green in the ferns in the corner:
the same ones that symbolize new life in the wake of disaster.

(she's still a new-born symbolist)

weddings traditionally are finalized, before the kiss,
of joint flames on a single candle.
try this at home.
please, do try this at home.
it's not a community center stand-up set.

held to the side evenly, neither wick extinguishes, but cloudy white
Perspiration strips the scrap pretense down.

musicians know the ability of affinity well.
you can't go wrong, the pianist says, playing nothing but C.
what ocean would disagree, her skin infinite kisses of molecules in
surface tension, their embrace protecting a universe from harm, from
sky-walkers that want to destroy and pillage perfection?

our sweat drips into the amniotic mirror of the earth's fluid body.
and sometimes we look into another's eyes and it just makes sense.

this should be enough to teach us to fall forward into affinity because we
aren't kicking away hard enough from that which doesn't understand.

morning in the afternoon

October 19, 2011 at 21:57   Medford NY

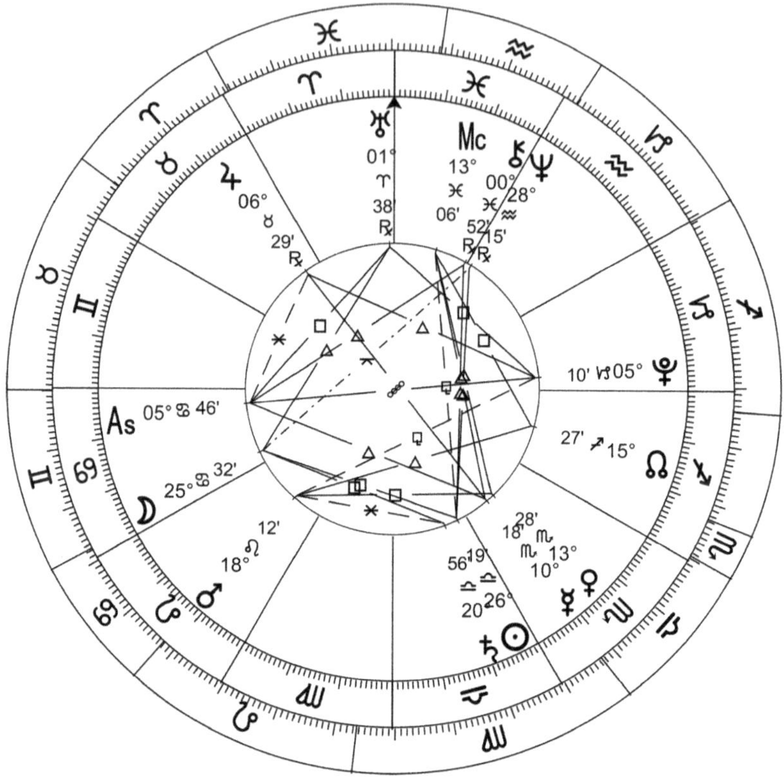

By referencing my Natal Chart we see that the most relevant factor is Venus in an extremely tight conjunction to my South Node, by one arcminute (a 1/7200 chance). At such small odds, Venus draws big attention to my past & past lives, what keeps me feeling stuck, and what I am letting go of, and somehow makes it beautiful or pleasing. The South Node is an uncomfortable place to be, but Venus covers it with a fine fabric so that it's at least tolerable. A Trine with Midheaven allows this to be easily expressed to the world.

This poem captures a time in my life of tedium, laziness, boredom, and feeling trapped in a too-small bubble. Yet, the South Node also represents a Gift from that dark place, so Mercury joining Venus there births a piece of writing. Moon beginning its Last Quarter reflects the emotion of letting go and accepting what has transpired.

14

I keep stepping in puddles in my kitchen on the floor.

my hair peevishly keeps falling into my face but I refuse to pull it back.
I'm a little spiteful that way sometimes.

there are two 1/3-left bags of bread and vegetables that haven't been put
away since three days ago. spite keeps me from doing that chore, too.
didn't buy'em, not gonna eat'em.

I start to feel like I'm in a cell phone video game.
one level that never ends.
the same task and the same buttons, and then after twenty minutes the
realization comes that I'm being a jackass and I slam the phone off. it's
not so bad to be on the train alone.

but for the first time in a long time it's daytime and I am alone in the
kitchen I grew up in, mine and not mine at once. I look outside the
kitchen window, a square camera lens flecked with raindrops allowing
me to be privy to the moving mist outside.

it's probably cold there. I consider chugging my coffee and diving into the
unmowed yard. like a wet dog I'd frolic in the wet grass, which wouldn't
take issue with joining onto me.

and then for a while I'd lay belly-up, then belly-down, then scratch
myself a bit, then get up again.

at some point I'd come inside because I need to pee, but I'm not really a
dog you see.

and I'm still in the kitchen, a box obscured from process. beams of light
get lost in here like rubber balls do in children's rooms or keys fall
through gratings in thunderstorms.

that story would take too long to tell, though, and my pan has heated up.
I crack an egg in it, wishing for hollandaise and wishing that I knew a
poacher.

defrosting in the brisk and saying yes, still

October 25, 2011 at 00:11   Riverhead NY

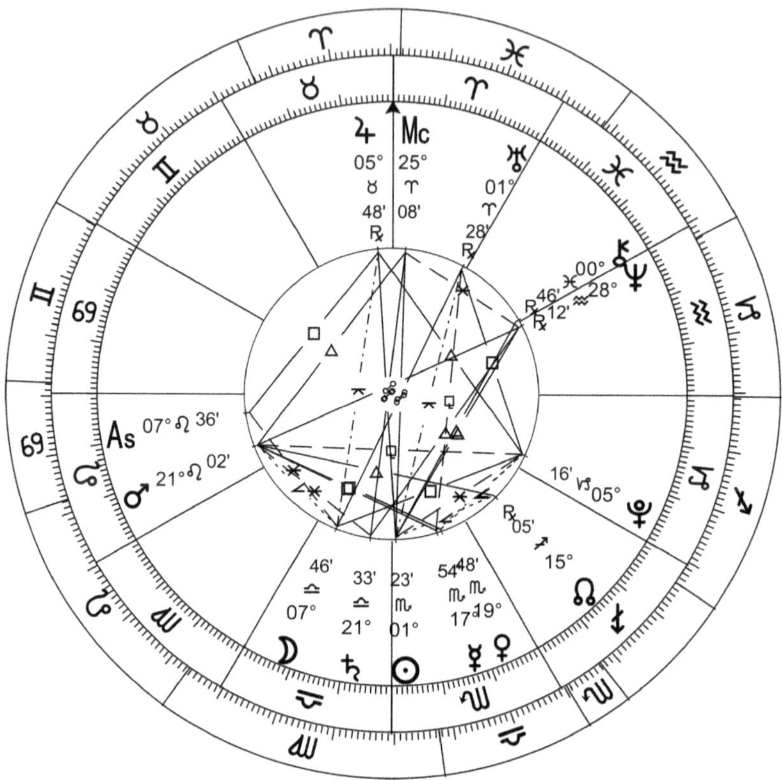

The amount and level of uncanny alignments between this chart and my own natal chart are significant enough that there I'm going to bypass discussing the poem's chart as it stands alone. These alignments are also the reason why this poem is receiving an extra page of delineation.

First of all, Mars is in conjunction to my natal Mercury by 2 arcminutes. Because there are 60 arcminutes in a degree, there is a 1/3600 chance of a conjunction of this or tighter closeness happening. Mars compels and drive us to action, and Mercury represents writing. In fact, I was compelled to write this: I remember being seated at the base of a tree and something coming over me that wrote through my hand. I watched the words appear on the page, and may have even fell asleep afterward. I didn't know it then, but I had fully channeled for the first time.

Yet, while it felt like the force that wrote the poem was not me, what came through was very much of me: after almost 15 years its imagery and message from the Unseen to my consciousness sticks with me as being a reflection of the some of the core archetypes and mythology of my own life experience. Some of the images actually came to fruition: for example, I actually did travel to all of the major coasts of my country of birth in a way that was quite chaotic.

While Transit Mars is on my Mercury, Transit Ascendant is on my Mars, showing that the essence of the poem has to do with my own inner passion and fire (besides the literal imagery of fire, which Mars represents at its core). Saturn (The Most Important Thing) is in an almost-exact Unx (Pattern Breaking) with my own Saturn, showing one last step to meeting my own karma. Saturn is also at my Imum Coeli (most private point) within a degree, demanding that I tend to my innermost experience. The Sun (Spotlight of the Day) is on my Pluto (Power) within a degree, highlighting where I show up as the most intense, and supporting an experience of unearthing deep experiences, even in the psychic realm. Venus (Beneficence & Beauty) is on my Saturn (Most Important Concern) by two degrees, and North Node (Head of the Dragon) is on my Uranus (Shock or Soul) by one degree. The Midheaven highlights my natal Aries Moon (my Rage). That's a lot to look at even for an experienced Astrologer, but here is a simple grammatical breakdown:

In that moment...

I experienced a powerful urge to take action (Mars) and write (Mercury), while my own inner fire (Mars) was being activated by the passing moment and my own feelings of rage (Natal Moon in Aries) on center stage (Midheaven). The Most Important Thing (Saturn) was my being grounded and facing my inner world (Imum Coeli). The light of consciousness was being shone on my inner process of transmutation (Pluto), and even the most serious parts of my life (Saturn) could be seen through a lens of beauty and the arts, in this case a poem (Venus). What makes me stand out in the world (Uranus) was in alignment with the overall cosmic timeline (North Node).

she'd spent years chasing bipolar Fire and Water both. The flame and the ocean, Dionysus and Athena. When one became too smothering, too demanding, she'd retreat to the other to beg for redemption, and both gods would provide in turn until yet again the other murmured out and she'd valley down into sanctuary again. Justifying with Balance and talk of penance she would place herself on sporadic coasts. Her dreams and poetry were filled with burning beaches, raging blazes gloriously consuming acres and acres, dozens of retreating miles of dunes, beach grass, poker-hot stones and shells. A devouring on the border, a silent epic war between the two cardinal forces was the oil, her arterial sap. At night the moon never waned as the months went by. There was never a change: this was how she knew she was dreaming. One last rite, she spoke when her voice could no longer cut through the roar and rush and din, and she acknowledged Risk as the possibility of Eternal Return. She could not bear cursing or being cursed thus and so made her way to the forest by way of a string.

Finding a root to rest between she wondered when the moon might be full again here, when it would be warm enough to swim like a wet fish again, to be slick, to float. She waited for a woosh to rip behind her and lift her up as a demigod.

& then the trees started speaking, cricking and cracking in layers. The forest creatures danced their scurry dance, showing off as the filigree amongst the trees' vast cozy stillness. she remembered them, her childhood friends, and the tale of the cottage in the woods, how she let that celebrated Pond dribble away, and she realized she forgot she had left someone in the bottom of the pot.

And right then, neither threatened nor threatening the lush earth mother with shade and moss birthed one more forest nymph, who you'll sometimes notice through licks of campfire flicking her wings in a stream.

animal love

December 2, 2011 at 20:31   Medford NY

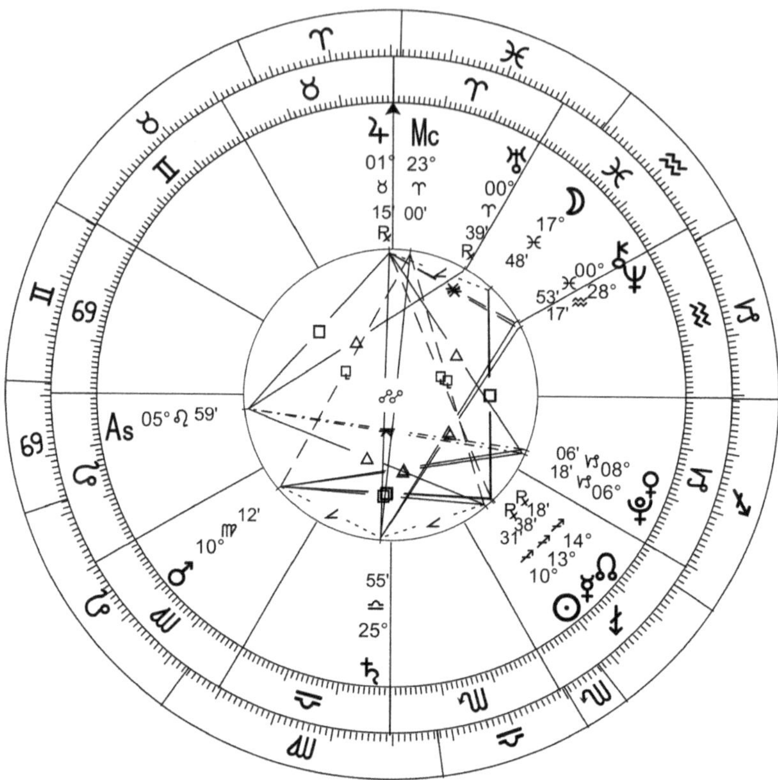

It's not shown in the charts in this book, but the Tropical Pisces Moon of the chart of this poem is in conjunction with my natal Draconic Moon, an alignment that indicates that the emotional flow of the moment triggered my Soul's intention for what it came here to feel. Besides that, the theme of water as mist or a fountain surrounding me is a strong Piscean (Mutable Water) image. There is a Sun/Mercury/North Node conjunction, emphasizing an orientation toward and communication with the Solar Principle, or Father (I speak directly to my Father in the poem). This arrangement is in direct alignment with my natal Uranus (a conjunction) & Sun (a trine), drawing out my inner Soul Spark. A Venus and Pluto conjunction in Tropical Capricorn, quincunx the Ascendant, creates a mood of soft seduction that feels unexpected but well-played. Meanwhile, Moon in whimsical fantasy-driven Pisces is in an opposition with a reserved Virgo Mars, activating a bit of "librarian lust."

looking up from inside of the tub to the fountain pouring down on me I don't see a wall but an oasis, a sun-shower marking the first warm rain of spring. the warmth of the sun in raindrops affects my body differently from that of the furnace-heat, even with the window open, sun shining at dawn, on those few mornings where I do greet him (father, I've missed you).

this might be the 500th time I've sat in this tub. I was bathed in this tub as a wee babe. I've bled in this tub, had teenaged orgasms in this tub, prayed in this tub, sobbed, sang, shivered, and slept in this tub. I've washed it and I've littered it with little hairs.

now I'm splashing around in it, celebrating the primal glory of having a bath. I play with my hair. I swing it to and fro, dangling and dready, ego-less like a cat bathing its OWN self like no one is watching (but we are, and but yet they're not in kitty's bubble) or a poor zoo creature stepping into a real prairie stream, and like an animal, I know love's essence.

on the side of a stream preening, guarding and basking in my own territory,

I wouldn't mind if you joined me.

on the water: a monologue

January 13, 2012 at 22:30   Orient Point NY

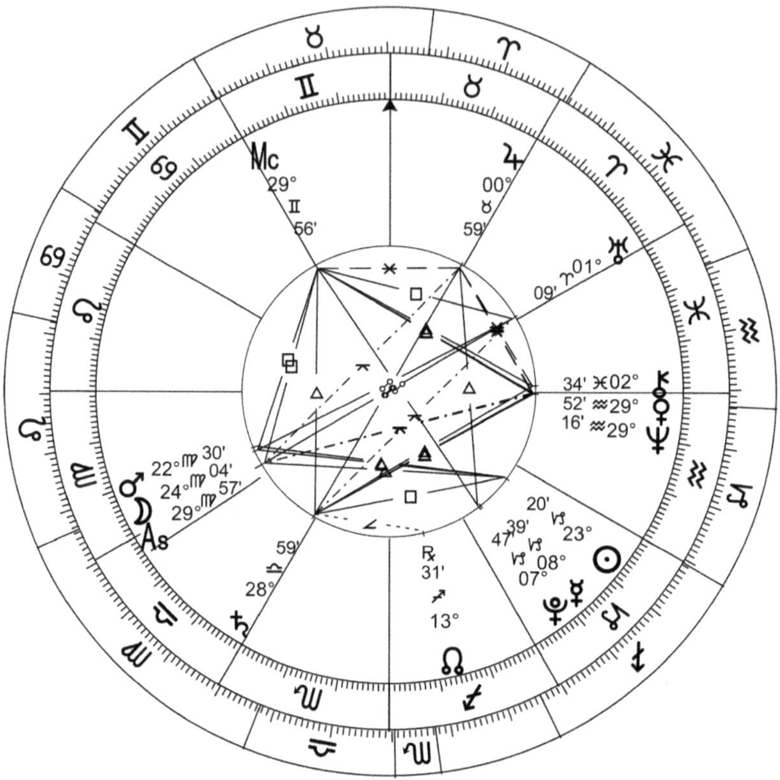

All of the angles as well as Venus & Neptune are at 29 degrees, the last degree in each sign. This motif elicits a "last push" bursting sensation, as though this were the last minute of opportunity for such a show of passion for the beloved. In fact, the speaker is quite histrionic and urgent about the display. Moon is with Mars at the Ascendant in an empowering trine with Sun, demonstrating the expressive fire of the narrator, whose feelings, though affectionate, are a bit aggressive and overpowering. Uranus opposing them at the Descendant adds another layer of craze over the other person. Venus & Neptune are the chart's closest conjunction, defining the phantasmagoric, blissful-agony imagery of suffered romance and forgiveness, and the surrender of realism for a phantasmagoria of images. Mercury has just passed Pluto, an also once-a-year happening that well supports the morbid introduction and lacings.

I am a fallen woman.

And if you died tonight, my love, I would sing a song for you. I would
wail a banshee call. I would wash your body, be your mortician in
shadow fishnets. I'd clean your body, and wash your heart, kiss your eyes,
close their lids, comb your hair, and make a pillow for your head.

These fears of death, my love. These fears of death and love, we cannot
escape. And this thing called new life, my love, is unattainable, for our
hubris has outshone the sun. Our hubris is struck down here, on the
water, caressing your body, with every movement, with every prayer.

In the valley of the shadow of death we have found each other. There are
no gifts that can be forgotten. As I preen myself and my flicker wings
there you are, love. Our creations together. I remember who you are. Do
you remember?

We are NAKED. And no one can tell us TRUTH. But RUTH, she tells us
to have RUTH. She tells you and me not to be RUTHLESS.
Fairy things tell me things, too. I was born to speak their language. Do
we speak the same language too? Is affinity enough? Can we be worlds
apart and still remain standing? And send each other sweet kisses from
inside of our dark, twisted sinews, our cages of bones?

I pet a bobcat and was caught on film. There are flying things telling us to
wake up. Wasps telling us we are alive.

Are we alive?

Do we dream?

Can I remind you, or you me?

If I were on a trail of tears with you, my love, I promise I'd watch for the
mountain lions too, and the rose tendrils of my hair would possibly serve
as warning but I don't know if they see red.

But I see red, devil melting soupy cherry raspberry red, every day, every night of my life. Crows cross my path and ask me to join them and I say no.

I say, crows, you don't see, I am Fox. Red tailed bushy fox, and I carry no disease. If you infect me with your scurvy, I will rage and pray to my gods the decay of your race. We are living in harmony. Let us share the berries and the offal.

Oh, it's awful! O, I am filled with awe!

I met Mother Mary and she taught me how to subdue snakes. She rained down upon me as I danced in fields with you, my love, and you my muse, can you tell me what to do next? No, don't tell me. Just keep breathing.

I believe that saving the world is a possibility. Through blood, and love, and filthy games, this immaculate conception, can we inspire the multitudes to see? Can we tell tales of saviors and gods and howl at the moon so she can send it all back to us?

If we ate of the Fruit of the Tree of Knowledge would we become like Gods and spew all over?

Our guts, our hearts,
they are fragile.

My bones,
they are soft like a baby's.

And I keep getting reborn.

I feel the vortex of the wormhole every day because

I know.

Because I have dreams of deliverance and remembrance.

Do you remember, love? When we knew we were creatures of the night?

When we laughed and felt each other's bodies coming alive?

Do you remember how we found each other here, how we betrayed each other? How we hurt each other so much and how I said sorry?

I'm sorry I've broken your heart.

Please drink this water with me.

I know that I am a witchy witchy nanana and my sins do not let me go on without admitting that you have saved me, and that I've taken your eyes and traded them for silver keys.

Is that what this is about? Silver keys?

I wear Amber on my Fuck You finger so that I can see. I throw rox in gardens and ferns into valleys. Tea into pots and letters into pails.

I walk like a farmer, bearing the weight of my pain, and your pain, and the weight of the world is pulling down. This grave truth I will never be free of.

They all want me to change.

If we arrived at a carnival, would you be my troubadour, and I could be your wench? Would we play with candles, and sip on nectar?

If I were spinning, would you grab and comb my hair?

But if I were falling, you'd catch me. and this I know because
you cannot tell a lie.
we cannot tell a lie.

I opened Pandora's Box. It looked like an oil slick. But here is hope at the bottom there. And I have found it.

airys

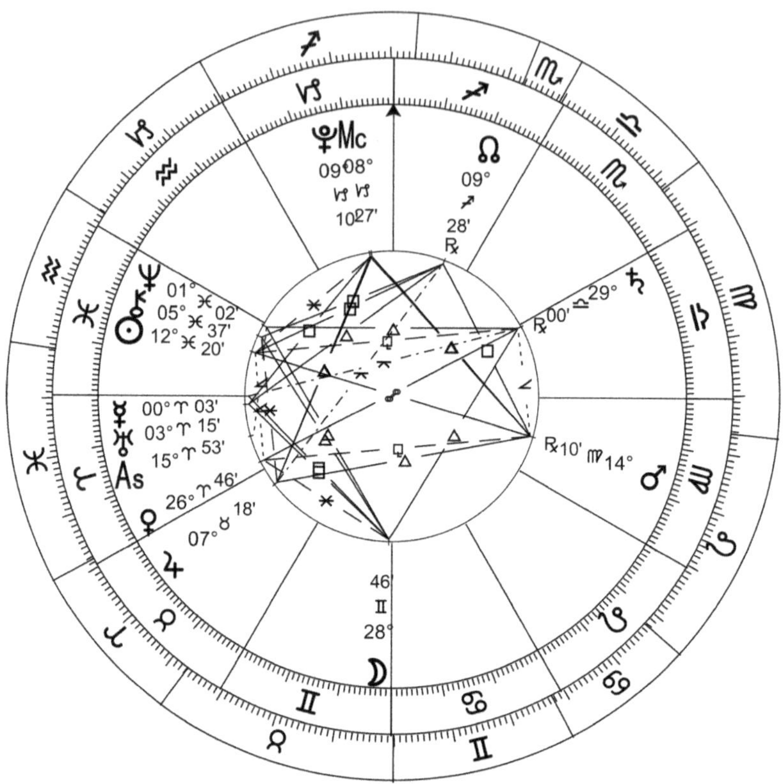

I'd been studying the Rider-Waite-Smith Ace of Cups (Water) Tarot card, which provides the core image for this poem. And yet, the title contains the word "Air" and is a respelling of Fire sign "Aries" on the Ascendant. Thus a play between elements is set. The eponymous Aries also claims four planets (including the constellational division), and Tropical Water is likewise extremely strong, with Sun, Chiron & Neptune in Pisces in the 12th house, creating the conditions for the spiritually blissful imagery.

Pluto at the highest point marks a moment of immense energy directed upward, reflected by the streams of water. Mars, the peering eye of the hunter, is in opposition to the Pisces planets and weakened by being Retrograde (Mars Retrograde is the most uncommon). Venus opposing Saturn grounds us: we are but physical, yet beautiful. Mercury & Uranus rising create a flash of insight: we are the elements intersecting, only models posing, and God rules the show.

the water flows up.

five streams.

and the dove upward thru the tunnel gods hand

god's hand

petals and rain plops flowing amongst the lilies and their fetal pads.

no peering eyes of hunters.

nobody's tying us to the trees.

the trees, they are wings in mountains.

we do poses.

on the corner of a cloud at the end of an island

April 3, 2012 at 04:01   Montauk NY

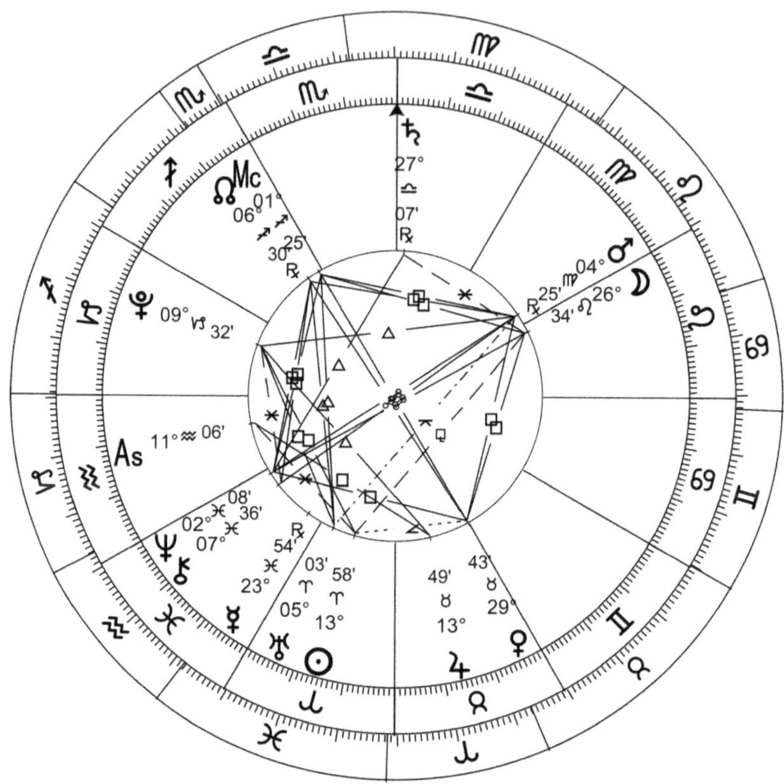

The closest aspect in this chart is the "Unx" (semisextile) between Sun & Jupiter here, showing a breaking of a pattern of belief about our Being: we learn of a whole new reality, and a false one falls away. Sun is separating from Uranus (who governs visions of revelation) but is still affected due to the "aftershock" effect. Together this arrangement creates tension and grandiosity that wants to make motion.

Jupiter is within a few minutes of conjunction with my North Node (Soul's Direction). Jupiter expands whatever it joins, really demonstrates it to the max. Of course, the content of this poem is a vision that I had of a parade demonstration of the fulfillment of the Rainbow Prophecies, a teaching that would prove to be central to much of my life in the years following. Tropical Virgo Mars and Leo Moon opposite Pisces Neptune and Chiron reflect the "marching band of spiritual warriors" imagery.

on the beach that day in paradise

the words came to us like approaching drums that didn't stop.

for miles and miles and onward into the sky
there were thousands of them:

uniformed marching in red hats and tassels.

wearing feathers and carrying skin drums, snares, rattles, timpanis,
wooden sticks, and metal.

dancing in chaotic tandem it snaked upward from a source that became
cloudy when I squinted to see a little better.

it was white, though, and clear.

warm and cool, breezy and still, silent and glorious.

looking up and questioning I turned to the side to ask you if you saw
that, too

but looking down I saw there was no more beach

and there was no more you.

and there you were.

by strings

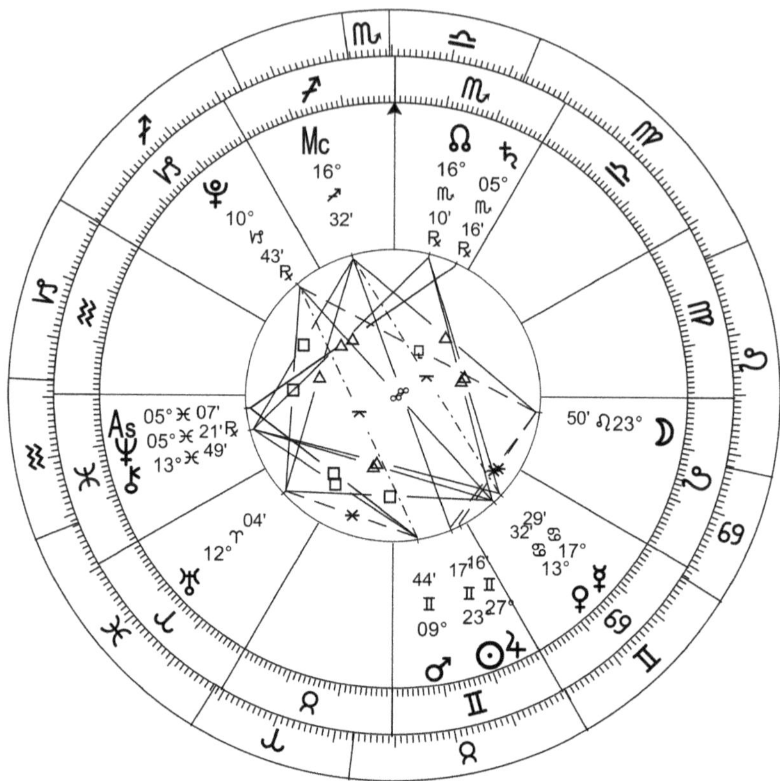

The key feature here is Neptune exactly rising while in an extremely tight trine with Saturn. Both planets are retrograde, which weighs them down and emphasizes the poem's sense of inertia. Neptune rising (with Chiron close by, emphasizing the Neptunian sense of suffering) gives the whole moment a feeling of passive acceptance to What Is. Saturn trining just within orb of the North Node (both representing Fate, in different ways) gives the a sense of Realistic Pessimism and non-negotiability. Neptune often indicates shifting reality, but here everything is ordained, pre-scripted. We unenthusiastically embrace it.

Moon in tight sextile with Sun lends a harmonious tone of "no resistance." Jupiter with Sun and a Mercury-Venus conjunction add benefic energy and the heartfelt hope of the last line. The latter two moving out of opposition with Pluto allow a sense of relief.

how can I say yes to that when I can choose right now to sit
in dim light
sharing space with the flies inside in summertime?

these flying things reminding me that I am alive,

buzzing me further inside.

reminding me

of the record left by my imaginary scribe.
of my trials and inevitable failures.
of my gems and illustrious truths.
of famous last words.
of epitaphs and wills.
of the binding nature of the signature.
and the evolving scribbles we make daily.

a standard black fly stomps on my hand.

my hand twitches.

the involuntary function operates without my consent.

without "me."

no command was necessary.

no imperative.

just the body moving perfectly with the ordained script of movement in

this given scene.

intuition is trumped by instinct.

I am a marionette. I trust that I am held gently.

forfeiture

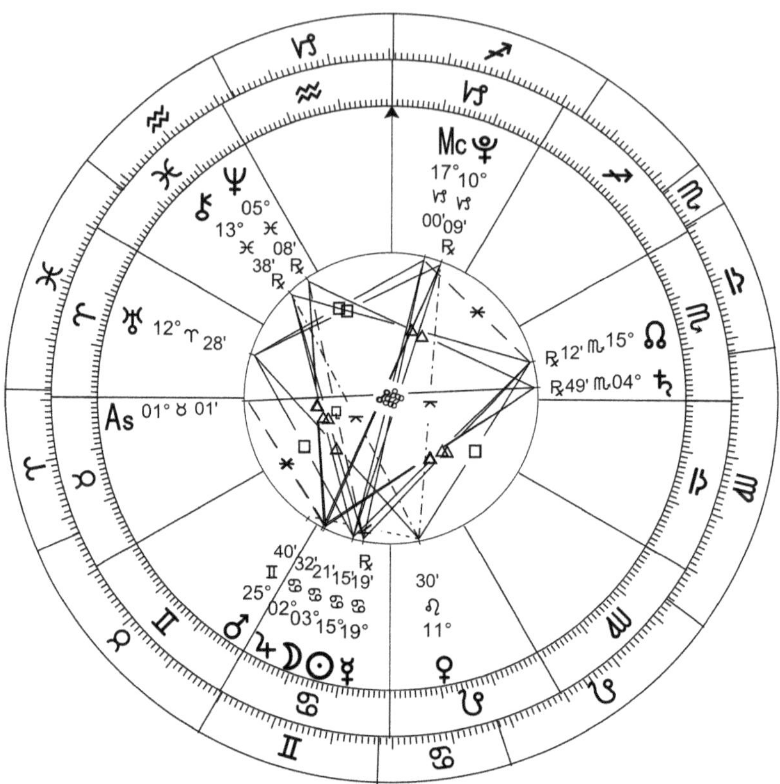

This is a "grand trine" (Great Ease/Blessings) & a Dark Moon (Elder's Wisdom) chart. "Forfeiture" has always been one of my favorite poems to perform, primarily because of the deep, stable, calm breath spoken to the very end that is required to finish it. Like the Moon has spent itself, so does the breath to deliver this poem.

The Dark Moon is deeply wise, as though having lived many lifetimes, & is ready to curl up & transmute with the help of Pluto (total transformation) at the Midheaven and focus of a Kite with Saturn & Neptune. These three together represent Darkness in different tones, The deep lightless stillness of the Moon at the end of its cycle flows with these energies of Finality and Dissolution. Something is over, being given up, & when the new cycle begins, it'll be gone forever. Each stanza is about the grace and lightness of giving up and letting go.

poetry is code for that shit you can't say outright:

it is a silent scream first,
an eloquent demonstration,
a ventriloquist's counterpoint,
A Majical transmission,
and a fool Devil's tool.

So pick a crusade. Represent it well.
then, please dispose of this note.

so says the zen master to the tramp:
truth and trash are one.
or, in layman's terms,
leave a penny, take a penny.
But really, leave it,
to be found abandoned by seashore,
friends with the starfish once again.

Meanwhile, sing a rondel.
pet a beagle.
experience instantaneous climax.
Borrow some fire.
be out there and harmless,
stationary under moving darkness.
Keep snake-spined and jelly-chested
Eyes like sand dragons refracting the wind in the grasses
like the breathing is in unison.

speak now, or forever hold your peace.

oroborus

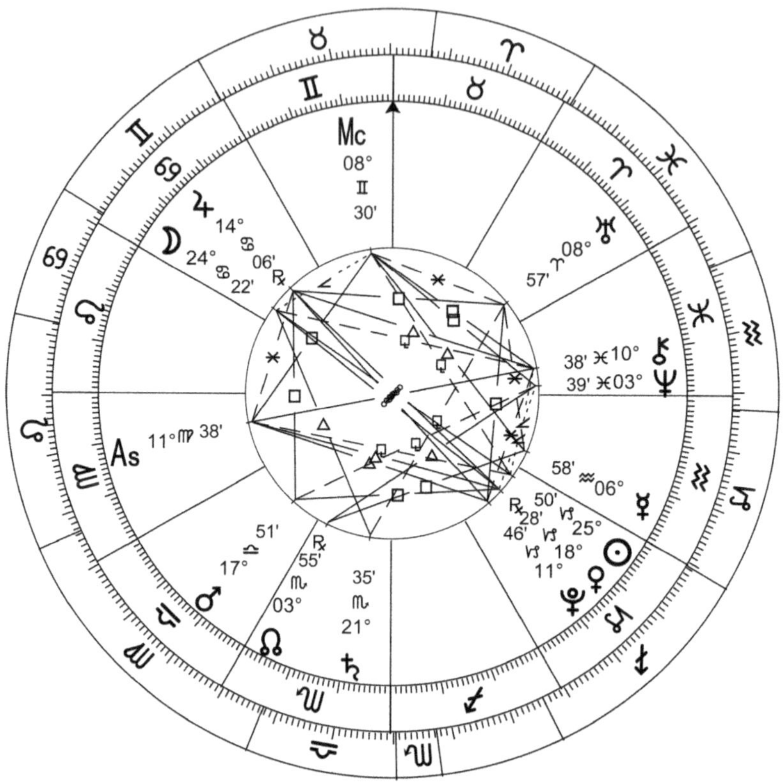

The Full Moon illuminates & calls out any shadow that has been lurking in the Scene that the narrator speaks to. This Moon-Sun opposition, supported by the two benefics Venus & Jupiter on either side (with chatty Mercury & impactful Pluto on the Sun side), depict a scenery of poets assembling & performing for each other. Meanwhile Mars approaches the party in an equivocating challenge (T-Square), pointing out the flaw in the feel-good scene and posing a bit of a rile. The challenge is mostly to Venus, who represents enjoyment. Indeed, the point is a bit of a bubble-burster. Chiron is on the Descendant: we can't fully enjoy it, but the wisdom is necessary. Saturn is at the exact arcminute of my own Natal Saturn here, so this was one of the iterations of my Saturn Return, the first one, & therefore this work is biographically notable. I unknowingly marked my first dip into Saturnian Adulthood by (ex)claiming the absurdity and the comfort of the poets' gathering at the same time.

following a period of nonmanifestation the fury of stagnant inertia
transforms to the self-motivated oroborus, the serpent eating itself in a
desirous auto-cannibalism of spirit.

Evolution comes eventually.
Crawlingly.
as we still cry for a Revolution.

Vaulted high, sizzling perfect lines are crack-whipped onto the page and
artfully articulated at the symposiums.

We are creators that DO.
A blend of starry-eyed fancy and spitfire catalyzes the quill.
Fronds weave wyrds in the air.
Listening in kind brings new association...
but admitting for good that the symbol is dead undermines the premise
upon which we are acting.
What I say, what you respond, becomes to us mere clatter.
Babble.
Chatter.
reflecting a moment that passes by like this one.

or this one.

And we are still here
playing show & tell
pretending in dim light
making beautiful things out of the pain.

<h1 style="text-align:center">always go</h1>

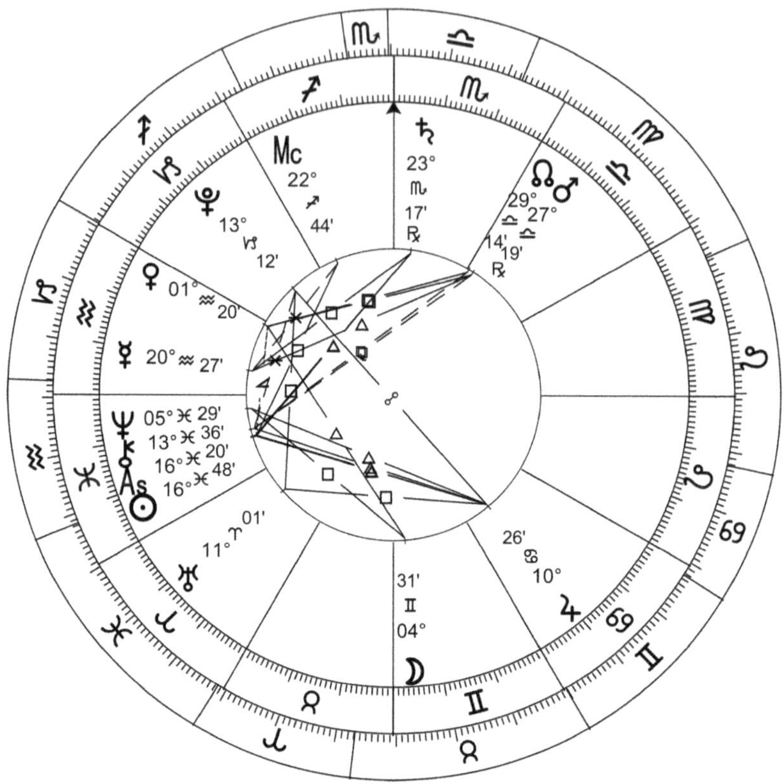

Due to the title and content of this poem, I'm looking for correspondences having to do with moving forward. Mars fits the bill, and what do you know? He's in conjunction with the North Node, which also represents forward movement, though more on a timeline, soul-path level...but also our material goals and how we achieve them. The Nodes are deeply complex and are a topic of great conjecture, but "forward movement" is an acceptable correspondence. Mars is also leading the way of the "train" chart pattern that we just happen to have here: most charts won't show this pattern, and to have this marching-on conjunction at the helm is quite literal. Additionally we have the Sun rising, a fine symbol for moving onward. Finally, biographically, Mercury is directly opposing my Natal Mercury: Mercury represents movement of any kind, and an opposition shows the geometrical motion of a line, directly forward, arrow-straight, toward the Other.

always go forward.

for Word

Fore! Words!

we form words

& note word forms

in a world of form

as wyrdness is whirled into form

jazz

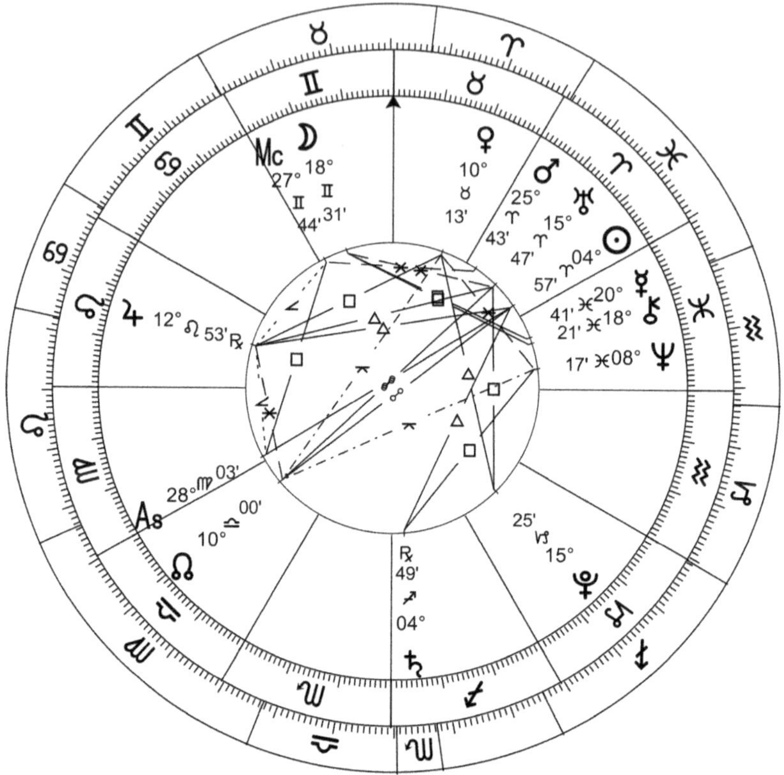

This is an action-oriented chart: Tropical Aries is strong, with Sun, Uranus, and Mars dominating the Descendant with a go-getter energy, effectively "getting straight to the point." Moon is the most elevated body, and in a matter-of-fact detached way true to Gemini, draws our emotional attention to what is going on in the public scene. She is in strong square (challenge) with Mercury and Chiron in the 7th: Due to elevation we can assign the main character "Love" to Moon, who provokes the thoughts (Mercury) of the audience (7th). Chiron there supports the deeper education that may hurt a bit. Sun in almost exact trine with Saturn in truth-oriented Sagittarius receives its zealous but realistic support in matters of living in authenticity & from the heart. Venus in her own sign Taurus & trining with the North Node in her other sign Libra shows this inherent concern for interpersonal connection being primary. In fact, this trine is quite tight as well.

Let's get straight to the point:

whenever Love walks in

the scene changes.

jazz twinkles and rumbles on the speakers.

finger snaps begin in the back quadrant of the room.

The walls grow gilded

and the trees remember how to dance

\

we forget that jazz is improvised, like life, when we are hearing it

secondhand.

do you know if your fish has been frozen?

are you living your life secondhand?

The electric organ holds the answers

Percussive, subtly but assertively, it won't let us forget

that when we cannot touch hearts,

we lock eyes.

i am animated.

July 8, 2015 at 19:40   Patchogue NY

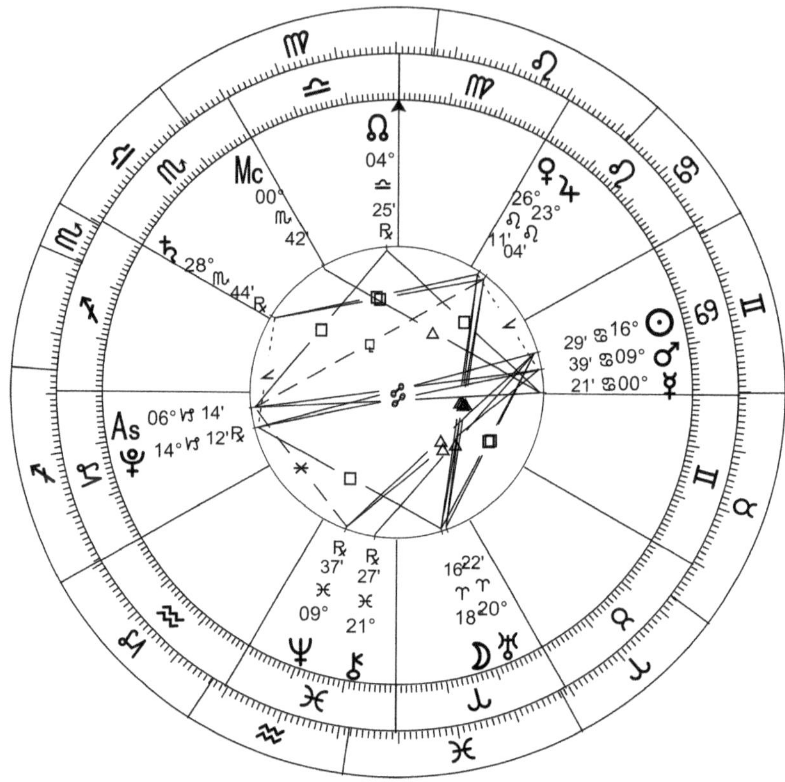

This poem's connection to my natal chart trumps any of the poem-chart-only factors: specifically, that Uranus is in conjunction with my natal Midheaven, a once-in-a-lifetime occurence. In my case, it was an on-and-off experience for a year due to retrogradation, but this is the only poem that survived that transit. I remember the day that I delivered this experimental poem for the first time very well: I had felt the ears of the Open Mic audience demanding a strong performance, one that would set me apart: I really wanted to hide (Uranus was in the 4th house of privacy), but I was being called to show up and stand out. Moon right there as well only amplified the feeling of being different and everyone being hyperaware of it. A Sun-Pluto opposition on the Self-Other axis created pressure to perform for the sake of the audience, and a Venus-Jupiter conjunction in the 8th house made the experience of diving into topics that would otherwise be potentially traumatic relatively easy.

I

I have been here before.

Where did I imagine this?

If they're waiting,

I am waiting.

I am seeing the red river explode in front of me and it is glorious.

My eyes are one with the fire, plasmatic & belvedere, attempting to

manufacture deja vu, to validate the nostalgia of our idyllic moment:

my image of you inside on the air deck.

chopped wood and slow water on the iron.

soapstone soft and waxy.

holding my stay

are lion, pegasus, rhino, and carpenter ants,

the last always plural.

my basin ringing

my pelvic bone resting

my memories conflating.

I will never leave.

II

Blessed is the monk who decides to move on but remain in the world of suffering.

The misunderstood Boddhisatfae can never claim hir claim.

instead, portrayed exclaiming,

complaining,

repairing

is what

this

process

is

why

i

am animated.

Blessed is the monk who decides to move on but remain in the world of suffering.

wanting winter

November 24, 2015 at 05:38 — Atlanta GA

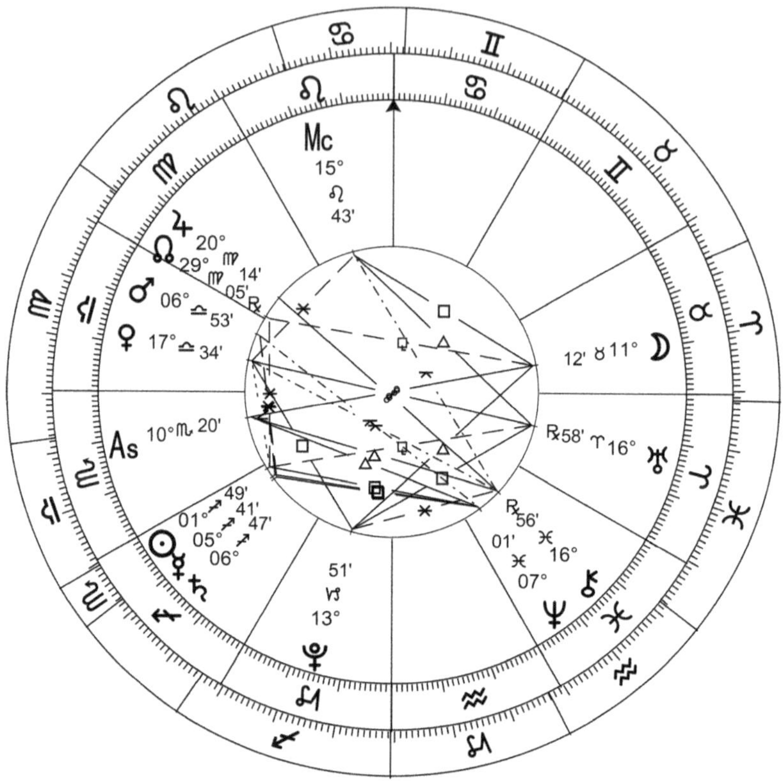

The extremely tight Chiron-Uranus semisexile does a very good job at
bringing acute pain into the moment. It was almost this close for a couple
of weeks, but it was only within a span of a few days that Venus opposed
Uranus (and quincunxed Chiron), allowing for a temporary reprieve
from the discomfort for long enough to channel a love poem. This same
opposition also creates the feeling of the electric romance experience
depicted: Uranus rules electricity. The speaker pleads for the cords to be
returned to their original positions; of course, it is futile. Pluto in a loose
t-square to the arrangement is responsible for the sense of powerlessness
against the forces of change. The Midheaven at a degree adding to the
aspect pattern allows the energy to release. Mercury is in conjunction
with Saturn, creating a sober, realistic response when the speaker realizes
that what they are yearning for will never happen. With the Sun, that
truth is clear as day.

is it safe?

To go back to the memory

of the place where we are always together?

Can we pull up that sun again (please)?

Plug in the cords that way again, please?

Or,

if manifestation fails in the face of change,

Then we will pre-tend

our garden

before it grows,

for freer to suffer after the snow.

The

End